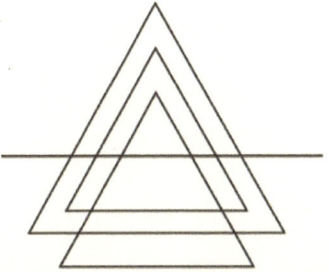

Vibrational Business

Vibrational Business

DAWN WOTHERSPOON

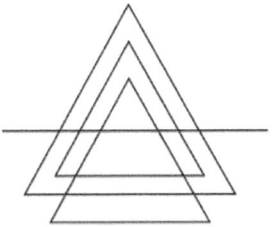

Vibrational Business

INTRODUCTION

I'm so honored to welcome you. My name is Dawn Wotherspoon, and I am a Spiritual Business Coach, Meditation Teacher, and creator of the signature programs, Discovering Greatness Within, and The Business of Vibration. As a long time entrepreneur and business owner, I've proudly owned and operated a brick and mortar movement and wellness studio in Saskatoon, Canada since 2005. I've been a student of the Natural Laws of the Universe for several decades, and although I can confidently say that in many ways I've mastered learning the basic principles of the Law of Attraction, I admittedly haven't always been consistent with applying these understandings to my own life, particularly to my business approach.

I often struggled with old programming and ways of Being in terms of actually applying this knowledge in a practical sense. So much of what I truly believed about business and money, was still based on old conditioning: patterns from my upbringing, paradigms from my formal education in business school, and emulating models from other business owners and mentors in my early years of entrepreneurship.

Despite my notable understanding of the Law of Attraction, for many years I continued to behave in contradictory ways regarding Universal forces. I worked ridiculously long hours and sacrificed self-care and precious time with my young family in the hopes to somehow magically create a successful business. I also grew increasingly frustrated with the financial results I was experiencing. After 10 years of existing in that cycle, I slowed down and asked myself: what am I still missing?

As I leaned into the practice of meditation and consistently focused on quieting my thinking mind and connecting with Divine guidance, I became inspired to revisit the Law of Attraction teachings and deepen my understanding of what it means to be a vibrational Being.

In turn, I was inspired to create this Personal Guidebook, which encompasses a collection of important Universal understandings and Guiding Principles for my business operations. I share the wisdom contained within these pages because as a Spiritual Business Coach and Teacher, it is my strongest desire to help uplift and inspire others to awaken to the truth of who they are, and what they're capable of creating.

Vibrational Business contains a collection of Universal understandings **for passionate, purpose-driven entrepreneurs** with a burning desire to expand their level of consciousness and learn how to effectively harness the Law of Attraction in their business creations.

This Guidebook was devised through me, but as a physical Being who continues to practice and play within the arena of business, I walk beside you as I continue practicing these Guiding Principles everyday.

Additionally, you will note that I've also included some reflection questions at the conclusion of each Guiding Principle section. These prompts will enable you (the reader) to begin the direct integration of these teachings into your own life and specific business.

For those who desire in depth coaching and valuable practical guidance on the implementation of the Principles presented within this Guidebook, I sincerely recommend that you compliment this resource with the companion, **Business of Vibration Online Masterclass Program**.

Information about this Masterclass Program can be found at:

www.dawnwotherspoon.com/thebusinessofvibration

My heart is full as you begin to explore all that's contained within this powerful resource. May you find joy and enlightenment as you continue expanding your level of consciousness as an entrepreneur.

With deepest love and sincerity,

Dawn Wotherspoon

GUIDEBOOK OUTLINE

As you begin to connect with the wisdom within this Personal Guidebook, I encourage you to take your time processing and finding resonance with each Guiding Principle. You may uncover value in reviewing the entire Guidebook in a steady and continuous flow, or pausing in between each Principle to reflect, meditate, and connect deeply with the teachings and reflection questions.

After selecting whichever method feels most aligned to you, **I advocate that you revisit this resource repeatedly.** It's likely that many concepts and ideas within this resource may contradict what you presently believe to be true about business, money, and the keys to success. Old programming and conditioning will often create an internal atmosphere of resistance, but you'll yield tremendous value if you allow spaciousness for processing, have an open mind, and practice patience with yourself.

Whether you're aware of it or not, you've been Divinely guided to this Personal Guidebook and the information contained herein, so enjoy the transformative process. Enjoy the unfolding of new insights, powerful revelations, and personal discoveries.

Allow me to introduce the eight Guiding Principles presented within *Vibrational Business:*

GUIDEBOOK CONTENTS

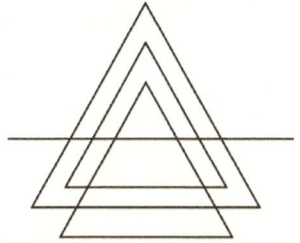

GUIDING PRINCIPLE NO. 1:

MY BUSINESS IS AN EXTENSION OF ME (THE VIBRATIONAL BEING).

Just as the Sun's rays are an extension of the Sun, my business is an extension of me. As the entrepreneur, business owner, and the leader of my company, I am the vibrational Being who influences my business the most.

AS A VIBRATIONAL BEING, WHO AM I REALLY?

During my journey, I now appreciate and accept as truth that at a soul essence level, all physical Beings are extensions of Source Energy. *I can insert any label or name that feels the most comfortable to me, as I connect with my understanding of the term 'Source Energy'. Ex. God, Goddess, Source, the Divine, Infinite Intelligence, the Creator etc.*

As an extension of Source Energy, I'm an eternal spiritual Being having a physical experience. Specifically, I existed before I came into the physical: I exist now in the physical, and I'll continue to exist long after my time in this physical experience ends. My body is my temporary home and a sacred vessel during my time here.

As an extension of Source Energy, I'm inherently worthy of greatness. I'm also deserving of unlimited abundance, love, happiness, joy, satisfaction, fulfillment, and financial freedom. This is my birthright, as I'm Source Energy in physical form. I don't have to prove my value to anyone, earn my significance, or wait for greatness. Anything (and everything) that I truly desire is available to me, and I'm already worthy of all that I desire!

REMEMBERING MY POWER PATHWAY

Quantum Physics explains that at the most basic scientific level, I am energy: I'm an energetic Being comprised of billions of atoms, and when examined under the most powerful microscope, my atoms are nothing more than vortexes (or voids) of energy. At my most basic scientific level, I'm moving energy. As an energetic Being, I vibrate (or move) on a frequency.

I'm a vibrational Being, and I exist in a vibrational Universe.

Through my eyes and ears, I translate vibration into what I see and hear. Through my nose, tongue, and skin, I convert vibrations into smells, tastes, and

14

touches that help me connect to my physical world. Through my emotions and feelings, I translate my vibration of thoughts.

At my very essence, I am a spiritually connected, eternal, and vibrational Being.

My vibration and frequency significantly impact the people, circumstances, and events that are attracted to me. Below is a visual reference to demonstrate this important concept: I refer to it as **my energetic Power Pathway:**

MY BELIEFS

The starting point in my energetic Power Pathway involves my beliefs. My beliefs directly influence my thinking. This interconnectivity means that whatever beliefs I've previously formed about myself from past programming and conditioning, these stories now impact how I view myself today as an entrepreneur and business owner.

To further expand this understanding, I reflect that during my childhood, life caused me to have a variety of experiences. As I grew older, I started to make interpretations, apply meanings, and create stories around these different life experiences. The meanings and stories that I created then launched the formation of my belief system. I continued to make interpretations and form meanings all throughout my physical life; accordingly, all of this past programming now profoundly influences me as an entrepreneur today.

Additionally, my past programming molds the level of success I now subconsciously *(or unconsciously)* believe is possible for myself. My past programming also shapes my beliefs about money, my confidence, and many other habits of thought, behaviors, skills, and personality traits I now carry forward into my life as an entrepreneur. The really good news is that *my beliefs are just thoughts that I keep thinking repeatedly.*

I am the physical Being who is thinking the thoughts; however, I am not the thoughts.

I am the thinker of my thoughts. I can change my beliefs by thinking different thoughts and reprogramming my subconscious mind.

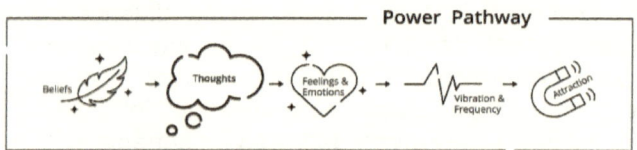

MY THOUGHTS

My thoughts (and what I focus my attention on) ultimately impact my vibration. As a creator in my physical life experience, it's imperative that I spend the majority of my time thinking and focusing on purpose and maintain awareness over where I'm directing my thoughts on a daily, moment by moment basis, as best I can. I can consciously choose the direction of my thoughts, and when I deliberately offer thoughts on purpose, I become the masterful creator of my life experience.

Before I became aware of the understanding that I'm truly the thinker of my thoughts, I operated in more of an auto-pilot 'reaction mode.' For example, when I'd receive a challenging email from a team member, or a customer complaint in my business, I'd automatically devote my attention to those things, and subsequently my vibration would lower. In comparison, when I'd receive a compliment, or a new opportunity would present itself within my business, I'd channel my attention to those things, and as I did my vibration would naturally rise. The challenge, was that I became like a vibrational ping-pong ball, bouncing around with no deliberate control over my thoughts or vibration. In this state, it felt like life was happening TO me. It felt like I didn't have any control over what was entering into my life experience, which was completely untrue.

As I've evolved and vastly expanded my level of consciousness, I now understand that life isn't actually happening "to" me; instead, life is happening in "response" to me. My life experience is a reflection of the majority of my thoughts and vibrations.

The thoughts I think right now in this moment, equal my vibrational point of attraction.

What I think about equates to what I'm attracting into my life.

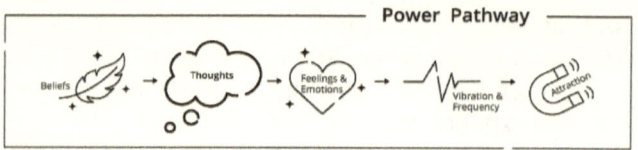

MY FEELINGS & EMOTIONS

My thoughts directly influence my feelings and emotions, which are specific indicators of my vibration and frequency. I know that when I'm basking in good feeling emotions, I'm vibrating at a high frequency. I also know that when I'm experiencing negative emotions, I'm vibrating at a lower frequency.

My guidance system informs me if my thoughts are in alignment with my desires. In short, my emotional guidance system tells me if I'm thinking in a way that'll allow what I've asked for into my life.

For example, when I'm feeling happy, passionate, and enthusiastic I'm in alignment with my desires and I'm allowing the Universe to deliver my desires to me with ease. When I'm feeling isolated, overwhelmed, or depressed, I'm not in alignment with my desires, and there's resistance on the pathway that slows down the receiving process.

Power Pathway

Beliefs → Thoughts → Feelings & Emotions → Vibration & Frequency → Attraction

MY VIBRATION & FREQUENCY

To reiterate, my vibration and frequency impact what I'm attracting. The easiest reference to understand the concept of vibration and frequency is for me to think about a radio signal. If I'm driving in my vehicle and I select 92.5 FM, I expect to receive the radio broadcast signal from 92.5 FM. I don't expect to receive the radio broadcast signal from 101 FM. I receive the broadcast signal that matches the frequency I've selected in my vehicle. The same principle applies to me.

As a vibrational Being, whatever frequency I'm vibrating on, I attract similar vibrations to me also on the same frequency.

This premise presents itself in my life as people, money, circumstances, and events.

MY ATTRACTION POWER

The powerful law that influences my energetic Power Pathway is called the Law of Attraction. The Law of Attraction is always present and always consistent in my physical life, just like the Law of Gravity is. I may not always be aware of its presence, but the Law of Attraction is very much affecting me every single moment of my day, similar to the Law of Gravity.

AS AN ENTREPRENEUR, WHAT I THINK ABOUT (AND HOW I FEEL) DIRECTLY IMPACTS WHAT I'M ATTRACTING INTO MY BUSINESS.

I stepped into the role of entrepreneur and business owner over a decade and a half ago. My initial inspiration to start my first business (a boutique movement and wellness studio for women) was based on my personal interests and inner most passions. I remember like it was yesterday. It was 2005: I was in my early twenties, completing a Business Communications Degree with a specialization in Marketing, and I was in the process of healing my relationship with my physical body after years of struggling with poor body image and an eating disorder. My inspiration for my business was to create a sacred and safe space for women to fall in love with movement again, for the simple joy and pleasure of moving and enjoying their bodies vs. transforming and desiring to lose weight. In the beginning, my business was very much an extension of me, the entrepreneur, but unfortunately that mentality didn't last very long.

The truth is, once I started my business, I felt overwhelmed almost instantly. I really had no idea how to handle the pressures of serving hundreds of clients and managing a large team. Accordingly, I did what I knew how to do: I worked harder. The harder I worked, the more exhausted and drained I became. For years, I made many personal sacrifices, all in the hopes that by working harder, I could somehow magically create a successful business.

What I failed to really understand at the time, was that working endlessly and sacrificing myself FOR my business was the actual problem. As a result, I directed my attention towards the external business strategy objectives that "I thought I needed to do" in order to be successful in business, never really considering how I felt as I did them.

In fact, I viewed my business as being something separate from me, and I tried to detach my personal feelings and emotions from my business, attempting to compartmentalize the different aspects of my life into neat and tidy piles. This approach was, after all, part of the beliefs that I'd previously formed while attending Business School. My training regarding business strategy was to omit my feelings and emotions from business; and at the same time, be prepared to work hard, and make sacrifices for the sake of success. So that's what I did. However, after years of following this fallacious cycle, I felt completely drained, frustrated, confused, resentful, and seriously tempted to throw in the towel. By operating my business from a place of sacrifice and obligation, energetically I felt horrible and completely detached from my original business vision. Besides, I was no longer aligned with my passion and inspiration: my vibration was rock bottom, and the financial position of my business reflected how I felt on the inside.

It took repeating those learning lessons many times until I finally began to understand that my business isn't separate from me. My business is an extension of me. My business is my creation (just like a sculptor creates a masterpiece). I am the vibrational Being that is influencing my business the most.

As the entrepreneur, what I think about, and how I feel, directly impacts what I'm attracting into my business.

THE UNIVERSE IS RESPONDING TO MY VIBRATION RIGHT NOW

As I embrace the wisdom of Guiding Principle No. 1, I acknowledge that I'm indeed the creator of my reality. I accept that all I have created in my life and business up until this very moment (the good and the not so good), I'm ultimately responsible for cultivating. I choose to be at peace with my journey, and I accept responsibility. I am where I am. Where I am is only the beginning.

From this powerful place of acceptance, I find relief in knowing that there's nothing standing in my way or preventing me from creating a very different future.

Today, in this moment, there's an opportunity for a new beginning.

The Universe is responding to the vibration I'm offering <u>right now</u> in this very moment, so I possess the ultimate power to formulate a new version of my life.

REFLECTING ON GUIDING PRINCIPLE NO. 1

Q. When I reflect upon my entrepreneurial journey, where has my vibration been landing when working <u>on</u> and <u>in</u> my business? Ex. Have I felt really good along the way? Am I often aligned, fired up, passionate, and inspired most of the time? Or have I typically felt weighed down with responsibility, obligations, and overwhelmed?

Q. Can I identify precisely when my thoughts and feelings toward my business started to shift? Ex. Did I feel inspired and aligned in the idea formation and beginning stages of starting my business? When exactly did that enthusiasm begin to shift?

Q. What was happening that contributed to the shifting in my thoughts and subsequently my vibration? Was it a gradual transition over time, or were there some bigger experiences or triggers that caused my vibration towards my business to shift quickly?

Reflection Tip: Exploring this shift in vibration can be insightful for the purpose of identifying how much positive or negative momentum I may have. If my relationship with my business just recently started to transition, I may find it fairly easy to begin practicing a different vibration. On the other hand, if the shifting has been gradual, and it has been a long time since I've really felt any positive emotions towards my business, I may find more persistence and focus is needed to begin feeling differently.

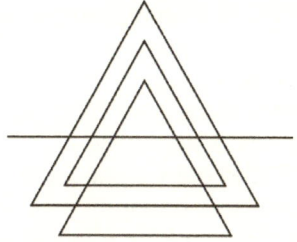

GUIDING PRINCIPLE NO. 2:

MY BUSINESS IS A CREATIVE PLAYGROUND.

I entered into this physical life experience to be a creator. I understood that as I'd emerge into this experience, filter through the variety of life circumstances, and lavish in the joys and challenges of living my physical life, I'd continue to form new aspirations, preferences, desires, and wishes. My eternal thirst for newness ensures Universal creation and expansion continues.

MY BUSINESS SERVES ME

I don't exactly recall when, but at some point along my physical journey, I formed the desire to become an entrepreneur. I sifted, sorted, and decided that being a business owner was something that I wanted to experience in this life. As a result, my desire manifested, gradually over time.

25

What I wasn't always aware of, is that my business actually serves ME (the entrepreneur).

My business provides me with another creative playground to form many new desires within myself. Specifically, the primary purpose of my business is that it serves ME (the entrepreneur) as a creative playground where I can expand, grow, learn important lessons, and continue to form new desires based on my experiences as an entrepreneur.

THE CREATION PROCESS

I'm a creator to my very core. I've been creating from the moment I came into this physical experience, and I'll continue as the creator of my life experiences forever more.

There's a 3-step Creation Process that's been working in the background and guiding all creations in my life and business thus far. Likewise, it's the same Creation Process that applies to every physical Being:

Step 1: I ask. I formulate desires, dreams, wishes, and intentions for my life and business, and I send those desires out into the Universe. I explicitly *ask* for them.

Step 2: Source Energy answers my desires. The things that I'm asking for (ex. an abundance of ideal clients; an increase in revenues and profitability; a dedicated and loyal team to play with) are instantly created in the moment of my asking. There's never a question of whether or not my desires have been created; on the contrary, they always are, in the very moment I ask for them. The Universe then formulates a plan to bring those desires into my life and business through the Law of Attraction. The Universe determines the "how" and "when" part of the Creation Process, as it always knows the fastest, quickest avenue to deliver those desires to me, and the path of least resistance to deliver them.

Step 3: I must allow what I've asked for into my life. I'm vibration. My desires are also vibrations. In the simplest, basic terms, I must ensure my vibration (in my powerful now moment), matches up with the vibration of what I've requested. When I'm in alignment, the Universe can easily deliver my desires to me through the powerful Law of Attraction.

GETTING COMFORTABLE WITH FOREVER BEING A CREATOR

As I begin to accept my important function in Universal expansion and evolution, I understand that I'll always be in creation mode. I'll continuously form new desires. As some of my desires manifest into physical form, from that place of receiving, new desires will begin to emerge once again. This progression forward is what expansion really entails. This furtherance is what evolution truly embodies. Since I'm eternally expanding and evolving, I'll always be in a position where new desires form within me, and they'll have yet to manifest into physical form. To simplify in another way, there'll forever be desires unfolding that haven't yet manifested. There'll forever be new creations underway.

This premise is important to understand because when I give too much emphasis to what has already manifested, OR when I place too much emphasis to the manifestations themselves, I can easily forget to enjoy the journey.

The CREATING part, of the Creation Process, is the journey. I'll forever be in the Creation Process; therefore, if I mistakenly wait to enjoy my physical life until something I desire has manifested, I'm truly missing the fun of being in the Creation Process.

Experiencing joy while in the middle of creation IS the fun part of being innovative in this physical life experience.

It isn't the creation or the manifestation itself that's the most fun: in reality, the ongoing creating is where the pleasure lies.

By realizing that I'll forever be in the Creation Process, and that new desires will always be unfolding within me, I can also allow myself spaciousness and permission to change my mind. I can recognize and honor the understanding that as I evolve and expand as a Being, my personal desires will continue to evolve. I'll never stop wanting more, or different, or expanded, or more impactful. I'll never be fully satisfied if I'm standing still. I'm driven by innovation; I'm motivated by a fire within me to continuously create, and so I can release guilt, shame or confusion around the questions, "Why can't I just be satisfied with what I already have? Why do I have to keep striving for more?" I now understand why I have to keep striving for more. I'm a creator to my very core. I exist to create. This is who I am; and only

28

when I give myself permission to explore the fullness of who I am without guilt, or boundaries, or expectations, I can truly shine in the brilliance of who I am.

THE CALLING TO CONTINUE EVOLVING IN BUSINESS IS TO BE EXPECTED AND EMBRACED

For more than a decade, I lived in the discomfort of misunderstanding the impulses and callings I felt inside to continue expanding within my business. I often felt guilty for not being content with what I'd already created. I wish so badly someone could have explained to me back then, that it's not only natural to continue feeling a calling to evolve in business, but it's to be expected and embraced. I recognize this message was part of a larger lesson that I believe I intended to learn in this life experience, so that I could become the coach and teacher that I am today.

Additionally, I struggled relentlessly to articulate into words how I felt on the inside as I worked on and in my business. I felt gratitude for what was, but also a strong knowledge that so much more was still waiting for me. I tried my best to be satisfied with what was, but I didn't always allow myself to fully expand, or dream big, or imagine life at its fullest. I think it can feel even more uncomfortable for those around us who really want to support us, but they don't understand the internal calling either. As physical Beings, we often crave security, steadiness, consistency, and reliability...yet creation is very different. Creation is wild, free, unlimited, fiery, messy, and magical.

When I finally began to really fathom that creation and evolution will <u>always</u> be occurring within me, and that I'll forever be forming new desires, it was such a relief. I ultimately allowed myself spaciousness to freefall, transform, and burn everything to the ground. Next, from the ashes, I enabled a new version of me to emerge. I allowed myself room to rediscover who I am at a soul essence level before striving for purpose or results within my business. In essence, I had to go inward before I could create outward brilliance in my business, and it was uncomfortable at times, yet absolutely necessary.

CREATING WITHIN MY BUSINESS

As I embrace the wisdom of Guiding Principle No. 2, I acknowledge that my business is a creative playground for ME (the entrepreneur) to continue formulating new desires, aspirations, and intentions. In understanding that I'm a creator to my very core, and that I came into this physical life experience to be a creator forever more, I can fully connect to the significance that all that I desire, I CAN in fact create. The possibilities are unlimited!

If I have the capacity to imagine it, I have the power within me to create it. My business can be a powerful playground for creation.

REFLECTING ON GUIDING PRINCIPLE NO. 2

Q. How has my business been a creative playground to expand and grow personally? In what ways have I felt creative freedom to innovate, experiment, play, and take risks, that I normally otherwise wouldn't have had the opportunity to? In what ways have I been able to give back to myself, through the vehicle of my business?

Q. By obtaining a better understanding now that the primary purpose of my business is to serve ME (the entrepreneur) as a creative playground, what interests and passions can I allow myself to pursue through the vehicle of my business? Can I identify additional ways that my business can further function as creative playground?

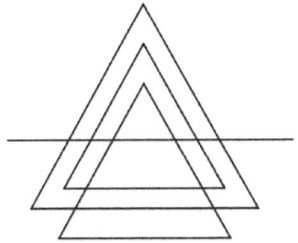

GUIDING PRINCIPLE NO. 3:

MY EMOTIONS AND FEELINGS ARE MY MOST VALUABLE BUSINESS ASSETS.

My feelings and emotions act as a valuable guidance system. They're an innate guidance mechanism that helps me to understand my vibrational point of attraction.

As my level of consciousness continues to evolve as an entrepreneur, I become more aware of my creative power and direct influence over shaping my life experiences. Likewise, this awareness facilitates an understanding of the valuable role that my feelings and emotions play within my business.

VIBRATIONAL POINT OF ATTRACTION

As a vibrational Being, when I'm basking in good feeling emotions, this sensation signifies that my vibrational point of attraction is in alignment with my desires. Simply put, when I'm exuding good feeling emotions, this signal means in that moment I'm vibrating on a frequency that will <u>allow</u> my desires. I'm in the receiving mode when I'm experiencing positive emotions such as joy, happiness, excitement, and satisfaction.

On the other hand, when I'm experiencing negative emotions such as fear, overwhelm, worry, or disappointment, these emotions are a signal that my vibrational point of attraction is not in alignment with my desires. Experiencing negative emotions is a signal that in that moment I'm vibrating on a frequency that cannot permit the flow of my desires into my life, and that there's some resistance on my pathway of allowing.

My feelings and emotions make it easy to identify where my vibrational point of attraction is landing, so it's up to me (the vibrational Being) to be deliberate about shifting my thoughts, which subsequently alters what I'm attracting.

MY EMOTIONS GIVE ME "IN-THE-MOMENT" REPORTING

To demonstrate the value of my emotional guidance system in the context of creating within my business, <u>how I feel is extremely important</u>, since I'm the vibrational Being who influences my business the most. My feelings and emotions are my most valuable business assets: once I begin tuning into this powerful guidance, I have the ability to make real time, in-the-moment adjustments, which will drastically impact what I'm attracting into my business in terms of people, resources, and results.

For instance, an example of this lesson relates to my formal education in Business School: timely financial reporting was extremely valuable in making timely adjustments to my business strategy based on my financial observations. My emotional guidance system operates similarly, with the exception that it's an even more powerful form of reporting because my emotions provide in-the-moment feedback.

My emotional guidance system provides me with essential in-the-moment feedback that signals if adjustments to my thinking (and subsequently my vibration) are urgently needed.

As I intentionally adjust my thinking, focus, and attention, I subsequently influence my vibration, which in turn impacts my degree of allowing. My emotional guidance system truly yields the most powerful and timely "reporting" from which I can operate and navigate my business. Accordingly, I reference it is as my most valuable business asset for this reason.

TURNING THE VOLUME DOWN ON MY EMOTIONS IN BUSINESS

Years ago, as I expanded my understanding of the importance of my own emotions and feelings as valuable assets within my business, I started to deeply comprehend why my entrepreneurial journey up until that point, hadn't really been very much fun.

35

For as far back as I can remember, I'd been trying to remove my emotions and feelings from operating my business.

I'm not exactly sure when I first adopted the belief that emotions and feelings didn't belong in my business. I think it had something to do with being female in business, and forming the unconscious belief that if I wanted to be successful, I needed to "think and act" like other successful business people. Since most of my past models of successful business owners were male, whose influence embodied limited or no outward visible emotions as entrepreneurs, I formed the unconscious belief that in order to be successful, I should turn down the volume on my emotions and feelings. I certainly didn't want to act or be regarded as an "emotional woman," because my past programming inferred emotionality as a "weakness" and a negative characteristic.

For the longest time, I mistakenly believed that my emotions and feelings really didn't have a valuable place in my business. It never even occurred to me to factor in, or consider, how I felt as the business owner. All of my attention and energy was directed towards other people, and I tried to remain very neutral, without allowing my emotions and feelings to direct my focus in any way.

In retrospect, I now realize that as I formerly turned down the volume of my emotions and feelings, I also turned down the volume on my passion and enthusiasm as well. My business truly became a vehicle for others to thrive and experience joy within, but it was all work and no play for me. It's no wonder I reached a point where I was feeling resentful and completely detached from my business. I literally looked at my business one day and realized that it didn't represent or reflect me (the business owner) at all. I didn't even feel like I belonged within it, and I'd built a brand and a program offering that was for everyone else, except for me.

From that moment forward, I vowed that I'd take all future creation into my own hands and begin building a version of business that felt good to me. I'd tune into my emotions and feelings, and begin listening to their valuable guidance. I'd also start making decisions based on the number one most important question I needed to begin asking myself - *does this feel good to me?*

VALUING MY EMOTIONS IN BUSINESS WAS ACTUALLY NOT EASY

The transition to valuing my emotions and listening to my feelings as guidance in my business was surprisingly VERY DIFFICULT to achieve. I held many deep-rooted beliefs about what I thought it'd take to be successful. Past programming caused me to believe that customers should be the primary focus of my business; and that pleasing them, and keeping my employees and team happy, should come before satisfying myself. For a while I wavered between trusting my guidance and falling back into old patterns of putting the needs of others first. In the end, once I began thoroughly understanding how my vibration affects my ability to harness the Law of Attraction to my advantage in business, it became much easier to factor myself (and how I feel) into daily decision making.

TUNING TO MY GUIDANCE

As I embrace the wisdom of Guiding Principle No. 3, I acknowledge that prior to learning about the value of my emotions and feelings as guidance, I wasn't paying much attention to how I was feeling as I worked on and in my business. Now that I'm closely tuned to my feelings and emotions, I can better gauge how good I am feeling on a daily, moment by moment basis. As I go about my day, when I begin to notice that my vibration is shifting (meaning that I'm not feeling as good as I was earlier in the day, or that I'm not feeling as good as I know that I can), I can choose to be deliberate about shifting my thoughts and focus, which will in turn allow my vibration to rise naturally. This mentality is what I refer to as "flexing my alignment muscles" which just means that I'm practicing and training my vibration to be in alignment more often.

REMINDER: I AM CREATING MY FUTURE RIGHT NOW IN THIS PRESENT MOMENT!

Regardless of my past experiences and all of the allowing vs. resistance, successes vs. challenges, and victories vs. disappointments, I'm creating my future right now in this very moment. I'm (in this present moment) writing the next chapter of my business and life story!

There's absolutely nothing preventing me or standing in my way of creating a satisfying, fulfilling, and wildly successful business, because right now in this very moment I have everything I'll ever need already within me to create it. I possess an emotional guidance system. I embody the ability to direct my thoughts, focus, and attention. I'm fully supported and loved by Source Energy, and I have access to the most powerful law in the Universe, the Law of Attraction, at my disposal. I can rest assured that I already have everything I need within me right now to create the future I desire.

REFLECTING ON GUIDING PRINCIPLE NO. 3

Q. Throughout my business journey, how much attention was actually directed toward ensuring that my customers, team members, and stakeholders were pleased? How much focus was directed towards me? How has this prioritization contributed to my present feelings toward my business? How has this mentality contributed to my business results?

Q. Upon acquiring a better understanding of the valuable role my emotions and feelings have within my business, how can I begin tuning to this guidance? What are some simple steps that I can begin taking today to start paying attention to how I'm feeling?

Q. As the entrepreneur, what I think about, and how I feel, directly impact what I'm attracting into my business. As I begin tuning to my guidance system and paying more attention to how I'm feeling, when I receive signals that I've shifted in my vibration and that I am no longer feeling good, what are some simple and practical activities that I can do within my working day, to begin feeling better? Ex. Go for a walk, have a conversation with a mentor, engage in a visualization or deep breathing exercise.

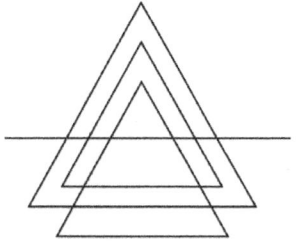

GUIDING PRINCIPLE NO. 4:

CREATING WITHIN MY BUSINESS IS ABOUT ALLOWING AND ALIGNMENT.

Creating is about letting in what I've already asked Source Energy for and reaching for thoughts that will allow the Universe to expedite my desires into manifested form.

I recall in the Creation Process, Step 1 is to ask, and Step 2 is where Source Energy answers, and whatever I'm asking for is created. As my desire is created, it's vibrating at the highest frequency. My desire is created by Source Energy, and it's vibrating on the same frequency as Source Energy.

In order to allow my desire into my life, which denotes Step 3, I have to maintain my vibration (as the Being who is receiving) at that same high frequency as Source Energy, so that the Law of Attraction can bring that desire to me.

This approach is what alignment is really all about - it's about pairing my personal vibration with the vibration of my desire.

Alignment is the practice of seeking to match my personal vibration with the vibration of Source Energy.

ALIGNMENT = DELIBERATELY STRIVING TO FEEL GOOD

I often try too hard and make much too big of a deal about being in alignment, because the truth is that I'm already in alignment often throughout my day. I'm in vibrational alignment with Source Energy and my desires, anytime I feel good. When I feel excitement, eager anticipation, joy, playfulness, fun, appreciation, freedom, love, passion, happiness, and any other good feeling emotion, I'm in alignment with my desires.

When I feel good, I'm vibrating on the same frequency as Source Energy.

When I feel good, I'm vibrating on the frequency that will allow my desires to flow easily to me.

Practicing my alignment really just means that I become very deliberate about paying attention to how I feel. Practicing my alignment means that I begin to rearrange my daily activities, actions, and efforts around one simple objective: feeling good.

Practicing my alignment simply means choosing to focus on feeling my best everyday, all throughout my day, moment by moment, no matter what comes my way.

PRACTICING MY ALIGNMENT IN MY BUSINESS

The same premise applies to allowing within my business. I have desires for my business, which indicate that I've asked (Step 1), and Source Energy has answered those desires (Step 2). What I desire was created in the moment I asked for it, and the Universe began conspiring a plan to bring forward those desires in the quickest, easiest way possible. In order to allow those desires into my life and business (Step 3), I must practice my vibrational alignment and focus on feeling good.

As I feel good, inspiration to take action will find me *(if action is needed in the realization of my desires).* Inspiration will flow to me in the form of messages, insights, ideas, and intuitive hits from Source Energy and the Universe. Inspiration to take action will naturally present itself. I reference this premise as the Universe leaving me breadcrumbs to follow. As I focus on feeling good and opening myself up to receiving guidance, I'm easily able to identify the next steps to take, if action is required for the unfolding of my desires. The pathway becomes clear and illuminated when I focus on feeling good.

REQUIRED ACTION VS. INSPIRED ACTION

There's a big difference between taking Required Action vs. Inspired Action. Required action refers to doing the things that I believe I'm "supposed" to do in order to be successful in business. Required action focuses on listening to the voices and the guidance *from external forces and influence*, and allowing their opinions and suggestions to condition my beliefs about success and what's essential.

What I know to be true is that all of the things that I desire in my life and business are vibrational in nature, and I AM the energetic Being who is vibrating and allowing (or resisting) them from coming into my life.

No one else can possibly know what's best for me, because they simply don't have access to, or influence over, my vibrational point of attraction.

Others cannot access my emotional guidance system, listen to the messages coming through, and then guide me on the steps to take to achieve personal alignment. Only I can do that for myself.

Others' suggestions and advice exist only as recollections of what has worked FOR THEM, not necessarily what'll work for me, because I have my own desires, belief system, thought patterns, and guidance system. No two physical Beings have identical vibrational points of attraction at all times, which is why I've often witnessed someone experiencing great success following one path in business, but then when others try to duplicate the exact same path, they fall short of experiencing the same level of business success. It's not the fault or failure of the path traveled. The results illustrate the reality that each physical Being has to listen to his or her own guidance system and take action only when it's in alignment with one's desires.

On the other hand, inspired action is different because it originates from guidance within. It often emerges as a result of quieting my thinking mind, and then listening to the inspiration that follows. Inspired action feels like ease, relief, joy, and happiness. It looks like fun and adventure. Inspired action is when I receive those "HELL YES!" ideas that send tingles through my entire body and cause excitement and anticipation to stir. I never have to muster up energy to take inspired action, since this is the type of action that I truly want to take; in fact, it exudes the feeling of playtime. This type of action yields the results I'm seeking. Inspired action is in alignment with my desires because it feels good.

When I perform inspired action, I'm taking action in a way that'll allow my desires to flow easily and effortlessly to me.

TAKING ACTION WHEN I'M NOT IN ALIGNMENT

When I'm not feeling good, yet I still force myself to take action because "I think I should", or I'm listening to outside guidance, I'm typically working in opposition to what I desire. Furthermore, I can recognize this resistance by how I feel. For example, if I'm tired and notice myself trying to "push through" the day so I can check off the items on my list, the more action I take, the worse I end up feeling. Fatigue begins to transition to exhausted. Exhausted builds to frustrated. Frustrated moves to resentment, and on and on until I admit that I'm miserable, and counting down the minutes until my day is over and can finally go to sleep.

Action taken in this downward emotional spiral is never effective. No amount of action can compensate for the fact that I'm not feeling good, and that I'm not in alignment, which is why working hard, slaving away, and making sacrifices for the sake of success never yield truly sustainable results. I cannot have an unhappy journey and expect to reach a happy destination. When I act from a place where I'm not feeling good, I'm basically working against myself. I'm better off just stopping the madness and going for a nap. I can reassess after the nap; and if I'm feeling good again, I can shift back into inspired action...otherwise I should continue flexing my alignment muscles and resting, until I find myself in a good feeling place once again.

To offer another example, when I'm feeling overwhelmed, despite the temptation to put my head down and TRY HARD to complete lots of tasks, it's important to remind myself that there actually isn't anything in that very moment that I absolutely "need" to do. Taking action when I'm not in alignment never equates to effectiveness anyways, so I'm far better served to focus on getting into alignment first and then taking inspired action, which will yield much greater results in the long run overall.

Taking action is extremely valuable, but alignment (feeling good) is the most

important first step, and inspired action follows.

SURRENDERING THE STRUGGLE

As I embrace the wisdom of Guiding Principle No. 4, I acknowledge that when a desire is strong within, it serves me best to release it to the Universe in trust and faith. When I find myself "strangling" my desire by fixating my thoughts on the "how" or the "when" details of it's unfolding, I can feel my alignment shifting toward desperation and neediness. In those distressing moments, I'm trying to control the outcome, and the truth is that the outcome and unfolding are not my responsibility.

It's the Universe's responsibility to seek out the most appropriate path to bring forward my desires.

My responsibility is to allow, by feeling good. In the releasing of control to the Universe and Source Energy, I allow.

"In this moment I choose to give up the struggle. I release control of the outcome to the Universe with trust and a knowingness that all is working out for me."

There's tremendous relief and freedom in surrendering the struggle. What I desire in this physical life experience won't come to me as a result of struggle and sacrifice.

What I desire will come to me as a result of making feeling good central in my business strategy. It's merely old programming that tries to convince me otherwise.

REFLECTING ON GUIDING PRINCIPLE NO. 4

Q. As an entrepreneur, what have I been programmed to believe is "required of me" in order to be successful in business? If I choose to focus on feeling good, then what am I most fearful could happen within my business?

Q. Am I willing to let go of control and wholeheartedly trust in Source Energy and the Natural Laws of the Universe? *As an extension of Source Energy, I am an attractor of all things required to be successful in business. As I ask, my desires are created.* Am I ready to surrender the effort and struggle, and truly begin allowing and receiving?

Q. In knowing that all I desire for my business will follow as a result of my vibrational alignment, am I truly eager to make feeling good central to my business strategy? Do I believe it's even possible to feel good as I create a successful and thriving business? Am I open to give myself permission to feel good?

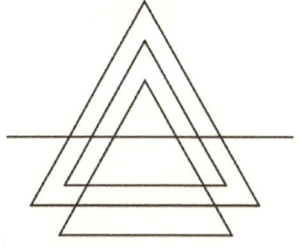

GUIDING PRINCIPLE NO. 5:

THROUGH THE VEHICLE OF MY BUSINESS, I BECOME THE NATURAL UPLIFTER THAT I AM.

I am a natural uplifter. It makes me feel joyous to contribute meaningful value in others' lives. When 'feeling good' becomes central to my business strategy, I effectively begin to harness the Law of Attraction to my advantage. Additional support, abundant resources, and Universal assistance begin to appear. As a result, I am able to extend my capacity to serve and uplift the world.

After my thorough self-exploration, I've ascertained that being in service to others is actually a selfish act *(in the most favorable way)*. What I mean by this realization, is that it feels meaningful and satisfying to help uplift and inspire others through my work. As an entrepreneur, my business provides an avenue for me to assist others, and I dedicate myself to this work for the reward of inner delight and attainment. I also recognize that since my intention is to yield good feeling emotions such as fulfillment, happiness, joy, and accomplishment, there's further value in remembering that the journey of working on and in my business should also be representative of these positive emotions. The better I feel as I work on and in my business, the more effective I become at utilizing the Law of Attraction to my advantage, and ultimately the more Universal Support I receive.

As I leverage this Universal Support, I increase my capacity to serve more people. With an abundance of resources at my disposal, I possess the opportunity to compensate highly trained people, invest in technology, and expand my business reach even further.

As a natural uplifter, the greatest attainment and contribution that I can make in the world, is to thrive.

As I thrive, I increase my capacity to serve the world in a grander magnitude.

SOURCE ENERGY EXPRESSES THROUGH ME

Just as I create within my life and business, Source Energy also creates. In fact, I was formed by Source Energy, just as every other spiritual Being was also devised by Source Energy. As a natural uplifter, Source Energy expresses through me. To offer an example of this understanding, I acknowledge that it was Source Energy's desire to share the wisdom contained within this Personal Guidebook. It was Source Energy's desire to uplift and inspire entrepreneurs to deepen their understanding of how vibration influences their business. It was Source Energy's desire to ease the struggle and provide relief to those who need it most. As I shaped this resource, the passion, enthusiasm, and excitement I felt within, validated that Source Energy was powerfully flowing through me as I created.

MEDITATION FOR COMMUNICATING WITH SOURCE ENERGY

Through the process of quieting my thinking mind, I have direct access to Source Energy.

As I deliberately quiet my thoughts, I open the pathway for receiving infinite intelligence and spiritual guidance. Meditation has been the practice that has most effectively supported me in quieting my thinking mind over the years. I adopted this practice many years ago; and I initially gravitated towards meditation for the benefits of stress management, ease, and the peacefulness I'd experience during and after a meditation session. Each experience provided much needed relief for my busy entrepreneurial mind. I wholeheartedly fell in love with this practice that I was inspired to incorporate this offering into my business, and begin guiding others in meditation experiences at my movement and wellness studio. I eventually started writing and crafting my own guided meditations, mainly for the simple pleasure and joy that it brought me. To date, some of my all-time favorite writings have been the intimate guided meditations that I created and shared during private soul circle gatherings.

Over time, as I basked in the delicious silence of quieting my thinking mind, meditation became a direct channel for me to connect with Source Energy. This communication emanated from inspired thoughts and action, nudges, and intuitive hits. New ideas would emerge as I meditated or immediately following a meditation session. As I tuned to these new ideas, I then acted upon them when inspired to do so, and this natural communication became a compass for living my life and building my business.

For instance, when I had a question, was pondering an idea, or encountered a challenging problem, I'd ask Source Energy for guidance and then focus on quieting my thinking mind to be open to receiving messages. The intuitive nudges didn't always arrive instantly, but they always came in the days, weeks or months following, and continue to do so now. As I've evolved and expanded as a Being, I now foster this connection and direct line of communication with Source Energy as valuable access to infinite intelligence and Divine guidance.

To further demonstrate this ever-present influence, meditation was one of the most powerful practices that I leaned on before and during the writing of this Personal Guidebook and the creation of the Business of Vibration companion program. In the years leading up to the beginning of this project, I'd asked Source Energy for guidance in assisting me to connect with an important message in which I could share with the world in written form. I felt a resonance that the message was to be uplifting and inspiring specifically to entrepreneurs, but I didn't have absolute clarity on what that message would be until I began setting the intention and asking for guidance. I opened myself up to the receiving of inspiration through the practice of meditation; now everyday before settling in to write, I meditate and ask for clarity and guidance. I affirmed my desire that I'd be a channel, a pathway, a faucet for Source Energy to flow and share wisdom and guidance through. I requested that the messages and understandings be expansive, revolutionary, and in no way limited by my own personal comprehension.

I asked that the Divine wisdom flow through me in service of helping the expansion of all who read these words. My greatest desire through the process became removing my own personal resistance, to in turn allow the guidance to pour through me. I practiced my vibrational alignment diligently, took naps, and used meditation multiple times daily during the course of writing this Guidebook, all in the efforts of getting out of my thinking mind and allowing Divine magnificence to flow. The result is that the words and perspectives contained within this resource are far beyond my physical comprehension at times. This resource was created through me, but also FOR me, as I continue to practice the Guiding Principles in my own business. I, too, am a student to the wisdom contained within these pages and likely always will be.

As I embrace the wisdom of Guiding Principle No. 5, what I presently accept as truth is that all physical Beings embody this same ability to receive guidance from Source Energy. As natural uplifters, Source Energy expresses through each one of us, whether we're consciously aware of it or not. There are some physical Beings who've honed and practiced their ability to communicate with non-physical energy with great efficiency, and I've had the pleasure of working with some incredibly gifted individuals who've mastered this skill. The truth though, is that we all possess this ability; and when the desire exists to foster our connection with Source Energy, it can absolutely be done, and we can utilize this power within our business creations when we open ourselves up to the exchange.

REFLECTING ON GUIDING PRINCIPLE NO. 5

Q. In what ways do I help to uplift others through the vehicle of my business? What's my desired impact in the lives of my clients, stakeholders, and colleagues?

Q. If time, money, and resources weren't limited or restricted in any way, how would I allow myself to expand as an uplifter?

Q. Which areas of my life and business do I desire more guidance from Source Energy? What specific questions am I ready to ask and receive answers to as an entrepreneur?

Q. What resistance comes forward for me when I consider adopting the practice of meditation for quieting my thinking mind? Am I willing to release the resistance (or learn to move through it) in order to strengthen my connection and communication with Source?

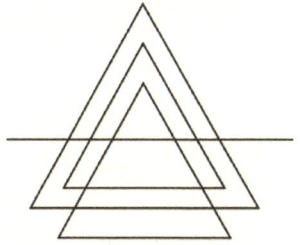

GUIDING PRINCIPLE NO. 6:

MONEY IS VIBRATION, AND IT FLOWS TO ME AS A RESULT OF THE CREATION PROCESS.

Contrary to my past programming, I now understand that money is simply energy. Money is vibration just like I am vibration. Money comes from the same place all other desires originate: Source Energy. It flows into my life as a result of the Creation Process.

Money flows into my physical life experience as a result of being a creator. As I experience life, I form new desires for money; and from those experiences, I begin the Creation Process. When I ask for money (Step 1), Source Energy answers my request in that moment of asking (Step 2), and as a result, money is created. The Universe delivers money to me (Step 3), not as a result of working hard, but instead as a result of practicing my alignment, maintaining good feeling thoughts, and holding steady my vibrational point of attraction.

MONEY COMES FROM THE UNIVERSE. IT DOES NOT COME FROM WORKING HARD.

I cannot emphasize just how challenging this Guiding Principle was for me to fully embody. For as far back as I can remember, my past programming taught me that money comes from working hard. As a young child, I witnessed my grandparents farm the lands and deal as merchants. Likewise, both sets of families worked extremely arduously at their crafts. I also closely observed my parents' experiences in their chosen professions: yet both never truly enjoyed their careers but worked diligently to provide income and pay for expenses, so our family could enjoy a comfortable life.

Coming from an upbringing where money was available but limited, I formed the belief that in order to get ahead in life, I'd have to be prepared to work really hard and make sacrifices, so one day I'd have enough to live comfortably. As I observed my parents' career paths, I realized how both had deeply subscribed to the belief that they'd work tirelessly during their working years, contribute to their pension plans, and set aside some money for personal investments, all with the end game of retiring comfortably. The ability to follow their passions, listen to their inner guidance, and fulfill Divine purposes was simply not something my parents likely ever felt they could really consider, even if they wanted to pursue them. In reality, they merely viewed work as a means to an end. Work equalled money, and therefore it was

56

something they <u>had</u> to do from their perspective. However, I honestly don't recall many moments where my parents referred to their careers with any real enthusiasm, devoted love, or pure enjoyment. They did what they had to do to survive in life. In many ways, they also worked hard in professions they didn't enjoy for most of their lives, so that they could one day hopefully enjoy themselves in retirement. "Work to live" was how I was raised.

As a result of my upbringing, I carried two very powerful and influential limiting beliefs with me that affected my money story for the majority of the first 4 decades of my life:

Limiting Money Belief #1: Money would come from working. It wouldn't result from anywhere else; it could only be derived from working in my chosen field, profession, or business.

Limiting Money Belief #2: Money came from working HARD.

Accordingly, I embraced these unconscious beliefs for the early part of adulthood and into my first years as an entrepreneur. In those days, I believed money could only result from the work I was doing within my business, and I also thought that I had to work really hard to for any extra. My beliefs affected my thoughts, so I focused on how hard I had to work, just to try to get ahead. My thoughts negatively impacted my vibration, and I remained on that lower frequency for many years.

In retrospect, I now realize that because I only believed money could come from the work I was performing in my business, I was resisting any support the Universe was trying to provide me. I definitely had been asking for more money and abundance (Step 1), but as far as allowing (Step 3), my beliefs and the way I directed my thoughts about money, actually prevented me from receiving.

This is why in Guiding Principle No. 1, I reference that the starting point for my energetic Power Pathway is my beliefs. My beliefs directly influence my thoughts, and my thoughts equal my point of attraction. My thoughts strongly influence my vibration.

Power Pathway

REPROGRAMMING MONEY BELIEFS

In order to think in a way that allows money to flow to me easily, it's important to create new beliefs about where money can come from and how it can flow into my life with ease. When I fall into old programming that money can only result from hard work, I shut the door to all other possibilities. When I fall into old programming that money can only result from revenues derived in my business activities, I also shut the door to all other possibilities.

The truth is that money can originate from an unlimited supply of sources, and it's not up to me to figure out the "how" or the "when."

My intention is to allow an abundance of money to flow into my life <u>from any and all sources that the Universe lines up on my behalf.</u>

In my Power Pathway, I acknowledge that my thoughts ignite a chain reaction that ultimately influences my vibrational point of attraction. What does this correlation mean? In essence, it's paramount that I have money beliefs to help direct my thoughts in a way that will thoroughly serve me.

To really understand this concept, I like to apply the metaphor of being like a computer. My physical body is the "hardware", and my beliefs and thoughts are my "software." In order to be a powerful computer in today's technologically advanced world, I need to update my software. Old software no longer serves me. The good news is that I don't have to worry about deleting old programming: all I have to do is upload new software.

Creating empowering money beliefs is like uploading new software. I don't have to be concerned about getting rid of old limiting beliefs. All that I actually have to do is continue to reprogram myself with new money beliefs.

REPROGRAMMING THROUGH VISUALIZATION

In the most basic terms, visualization is imagining a story of what I want to experience. Visualization is the process of having a "movie" or "story" play out in my mind. Through the process of having this picture play out in my mind repeatedly, I can reprogram my subconscious mind and create new money beliefs.

I can convey this concept when thinking about competitive sports or dance, where athletes visualize themselves performing at their peak states. They mentally prepare how they want their events to go, by going over and over again in their minds how they'll succeed. This strategy works because the same parts of the brain are activated by imagining doing something, as are motivated when actually doing it.

With enough repetition, I can form new neural pathways in my brain, which in turn become my new beliefs. It doesn't matter to my subconscious mind if the story that I am imagining is "true." My subconscious mind actually can't tell the difference between "real" and "imagined." In my visualizations I can focus on creating a story of the future me: the version of me that I am becoming; the version of me who allows money and abundance to flow very easily; the version of me who is already wealthy, abundant, and prosperous.

WHAT EXACTLY AM I REPROGRAMMING?

I begin by reprogramming how money can flow into my life.

I desire the Universe to bring forward an abundance of money from <u>any</u> and <u>all</u> sources that it coordinates on my behalf.

The Universe is the master orchestrator of putting together all the puzzle pieces, so it's not my responsibility to contemplate or try to dictate "how" money can or will flow into my life. In fact, I couldn't fathom all the possibilities, even if I tried, but the good news is that I don't have to as the Universe is doing that for me. I'll accept and allow an abundance of money from any and all sources the Universe brings forward for me.

The second aspect I am reprogramming is accepting "why" money will flow into my life.

I desire an abundance of money to flow into my physical life <u>simply as a result of feeling good.</u>

Since I can ask for anything - I desire the Universe to deliver an abundance of money to me, simply in exchange for feeling good. When I feel good, I'm allowing money to flow into my life easily and effortlessly; and since I can ask for anything, it's also my desire that money flows quickly in and slowly out, creating a surplus of wealth and prosperity in my bank accounts.

The third belief that I am reprogramming is how I want to feel as money flows in and out of my life naturally.

I desire to feel grateful and satisfied as money flows into my life, knowing that I am the creator who brought forward that manifestation. I seek to feel inner peace and appreciation as money flows out of my life, honoring the beauty that there's an unlimited supply of money available to me. Then as I release money back into the Universe, I accept that more is already on its way to me.

WHEN I'M EXPERIENCING FEAR, WORRY, OR THOUGHTS OF LACK ABOUT MONEY

When I'm feeling resistance around money, which in the past has shown as feelings of fear, worry, scarcity, and lack, there are some significant steps that I can take to slow the negative momentum. First off, it's beneficial to try my very best to catch myself in the early stages of feeling the resistance. As I tune to my emotions and feelings more often throughout my day, I can usually *feel the shifting occurring*. It most often occurs in response to something that has triggered me, such as a bill or invoice showing up in my inbox or mailbox, or the start of a new month approaching (which is when most of my bills are due). Regardless of what causes the trigger, as soon as the awareness takes shape, I can recognize that it's time to become deliberate about gently shifting my thoughts towards better feeling thoughts about money.

Similarly, I know from experience, that in the very moment of resistance, it's highly unlikely I'll be able to shift from fear or worry, to feeling the emotions of abundance or joy. That's really asking too much of myself, to try to muster up super joyous feelings in a time when I'm experiencing the exact opposite. So my aim in those resistant moments becomes simply to feel more at ease and to find relief from those worrisome thoughts. I do that by quieting my thinking mind for a few moments either through a meditation, or focusing on relaxed breathing. Once I can feel myself settling into my body and returning back into present moment awareness, I gently remind myself of what I know to be true about money. I write in my journal or repeat affirming statements in my head, such as:

→ Money is vibration, just as I am vibration.

→ Money comes from the Universe.

→ Right now in this moment, I desire an abundance of money to flow into my life. I have asked, and I know that Source Energy has answered this request, and the Universe is plotting the path of least resistance to bring an abundance of money into my life. This process doesn't have to take a long time; in fact, it can happen very quickly as the Universe is very powerful.

→ I trust the Natural Laws of the Universe.

→ My role is to allow the money into my life, and it flows most powerfully when I feel good. An abundance of money flows into my life simply as a result of feeling good.

→ In this very moment, I choose to focus my attention on feeling good. I will look for things to feel good about, and I'll find them.

→ I already feel a sense of calm coming over me as I summon my beliefs about money. I'm not alone in this journey. Source Energy is always with me, creating all that I ask for. The Universe is always with me, continually responding to my vibration.

→ I already have all that I'll ever need, right now in this moment, to allow an abundance of money to flow into my life, and I'm doing it right now.

→ I'm practicing my alignment. I'm shifting my thoughts, so that I can feel a profound sense of relief and ease. I love the feeling of ease.

→ It feels good to trust. It feels good to release this weight off my chest and shoulders. It feels good to welcome the lightness within me once again.

THINKING ON PURPOSE

As I embrace the wisdom of Guiding Principle No. 6, I acknowledge the power of gently reminding myself of what I already believe to be true about money. This practice helps me return to feelings of ease and peace; and from that place of relief, I then can begin focusing on feeling even better as I go about my day. I can begin reaching for thoughts that will help me create feelings of optimism, hopefulness, and eventually appreciation and joy. This practice of deliberate thinking is critical if I desire to allow the flow of money into my life.

I also find immense value in utilizing the repetition of money mantras throughout my day as statements of inspiration that help direct my thinking. *Some of my personal favorite Money Mantras include:*
- → Money flows to me, simply as a result of feeling good.
- → There's an abundance of money on its way to me right now.
- → There's lots of money available for me right now.
- → Today I'll look for things to feel good about and I'll find them.
- → I choose happiness and joy today, knowing that abundance is on its way to me right now in this very moment.

REFLECTING ON GUIDING PRINCIPLE NO. 6

Q. In my business right now, do I believe I have to work hard for money? Do I feel that success comes from sacrifice and working long, hard hours? What stories have I created about where the money comes from, and what's possible for me in business?

Q. How can I begin the process of reprogramming my subconscious mind? Am I willing to explore techniques such as visualization, hypnosis, using affirmations, and deliberate thinking?

GUIDING PRINCIPLE NO. 7:

VIBRATIONAL MARKETING CENTERS ON ME, NOT MY CUSTOMERS.

The marketing campaign that I'm launching is not to attract my ideal clients to my products and services, as they've already been attracted and gathered. Instead, it serves to attract me there: to bring me into vibrational alignment with what has already been created on my behalf.

APPLYING THE CREATION PROCESS TO MARKETING WITHIN MY BUSINESS

As far as the marketing, promoting, and selling of my products and services within my business, the first step is always for me to ask Source Energy for what I want. Answering the question: right now in this moment, what do I desire to create within my business?

THE DIFFERENCE BETWEEN GENERAL VS. SPECIFIC ASKING

It's essential to note that in the asking step, if I become overly detailed and too specific about my desire and this causes me to feel overwhelmed or doubtful, because I don't know "how" or "when" my desire will come, and I can't see a natural path to it's manifestation, I'm better off asking in general terms. For example, instead of setting specific numbers, benchmarks, or goals with firm deadlines, I can ask for "an abundance of clients," "lots of money flowing into my business," or "extra unexpected income in my business bank account." I understand that it's not actually the words or the specific details that matter most in the Creation Process, as the Universe responds to my vibration.

My emotional guidance system always and consistently provides me feedback regarding which method of asking is best for where I'm at in my journey. To offer another example, I can acknowledge that goal setting with rigid time deadlines has never really felt in alignment for me. Historically, if I were to set a benchmark or goal to achieve x-number of dollars or sales by a certain date, by focusing on the specifics of that desire, I often could feel myself shifting out of alignment. I would habitually end up breaking down the timeline of that goal into months, weeks, and days, and as I did this, my emotional guidance system would immediately express signals of overwhelm, anxiousness, and uncertainty. This internal feedback was always consistent, and so I've learned that the most ideal type of asking and goal setting for me, is to be general in what I desire. I now ask for what I desire in more basic terms, knowing that I can release my desires to Source

Energy, and the Universe will determine the exact details of its magnitude and the process of its unfolding. I detach from the specifics, and as I do, I feel an immediate sense of ease and relief. These emotions are validation from my guidance system that this general approach to asking is most in alignment for me.

CREATING FROM THIS MOMENT FORWARD

In the asking (Step 1), it's also important that I refrain from allowing past results and experiences to dictate or influence what I allow myself to ask for in this powerful now moment.

My past results are merely a reflection of my vibrational alignment and degree of allowing.

Today, in this very moment, it's a new beginning and a fresh opportunity to create from this moment forward. Today I'm creating my future, and the truth is that anything is possible.

It's beneficial when I allow myself the opportunity to think big and actually desire what I want in the fullest sense, and not limit myself to just ask for more of the same or what I deem as "reasonable" or "realistic." To achieve this growth, I can ask myself, what do I really want at this point in my journey? I can even go as far to question myself, what would really surprise and delight me? What would really knock my socks off? What would be fun and amazing to create within my business?

There's immense relief in allowing myself to ask and create from this present moment.

It's an opportunity to press the reset button on everything that has occurred prior, and I allow myself a fresh slate and blank canvas to create from accordingly.

Step 2 in the Creation Process: Source Energy answers my request, and my desires are instantly created. The Universe gathers and assembles all ideal clients who are seeking the kind of products, services, and support that I can specifically provide. On the receiving end, it's critical to note that my ideal clients have already asked for what I'm offering. They've also used the Creation Process on their end, either consciously or unconsciously, and they've asked Source Energy for what they desire, (which is perfectly aligned with what I'm providing). We're already a perfect match!

Through the Law of Attraction, the Universe finds the most ideal vibrational matches for what I'm offering, and it does this automatically on my behalf. Vibrationally, everything is lined up, and the Universe then looks for the path of least resistance to bring my ideal clients and me together. The creation part of the process is complete. The attraction part of the process is also finished. The clients have already been assembled. What I desire has already been created, even though I can't yet see it in manifested form. How long it takes to physically manifest only depends on one thing - my vibrational alignment with my ideal clients.

Step 3 in the Creation Process: I must move into vibrational alignment with my desires. As a vibrational

Being, in order to allow what I've asked for into my business experience, I must deliberately align my vibration with the vibration of my desires. Since alignment is an ongoing practice, and I am forever fluxing in and out of alignment throughout my day, my "work" in the Creation Process becomes deliberately practicing my alignment as best I can. Expressed another way, my "work" in the Creation Process is to simply focus on feeling good and allow all that I'm desiring to flow into my life and business.

MARKETING TO MAKE ME FEEL GOOD

Since my ideal clients, money, and revenue I'm desiring for my business have already been lined up for me by Universal forces, marketing and promotions now take on a new purpose. All of my outward marketing efforts now just have a singular focus: to help me maintain alignment with my desires. In short, all of my marketing efforts aim at helping me (the entrepreneur) feel good. When feeling good, I maintain my alignment and enable Universal Support to bring forward what I've been requesting.
The marketing campaigns I launch are simply a way for me to get excited, enthusiastic, and thrilled about the products and services I'm offering. My marketing activities serve to remind me how wonderful it feels to share my services with others that are already on their way to me. Marketing now takes on the purpose of helping me feel really good about what I'm delivering. As my excitement increases, I vibrationally align with what I am seeking, and I allow all my desires to flow into my business.

WHY MARKETING FROM A PLACE OF NOTICING LACK NEVER WORKS

I previously viewed marketing as a means or method of drawing clients into my business. I carried around the misguided limiting belief that in order to have a successful business, it was up to ME (the business owner) to attract and lure clients to my business. Upon reflection, I was attempting to do the job of the Universe. I was trying to find and coax ideal clients my way, which I now understand isn't my role in the Creation Process. What's worse, I was also viewing my marketing efforts from the vantage point of what was *missing* in my business. Meaning, I was noticing what was lacking in my business (the number of ideal clients and/or the revenue numbers I wanted). Then from that place of noticing the void, I then offered marketing efforts to try to attract and draw clients into my business to eliminate the lack.

Offering marketing efforts from a place of noticing lack only attracts more lack.

So, despite my best attempts at creating really innovative and exciting marketing campaigns, promotions, and offerings, I often didn't see the results I was desiring. I now better understand my place in the Creation Process is not to attract and lure ideal clients my way. It's the responsibility of Source Energy and the Universe to gather and assemble my ideal clients. In fact, the gathering has already been addressed. What I want is already done; it's not missing or lacking in anyway. I'm not in the process of creating it now, since it has already been created (this is what Step 2 really represents). My only responsibility becomes allowing what the Universe has already lined up for me into my life and business.

REPROGRAMMING MY BELIEFS AROUND MARKETING

My formal Business School education background was based in traditional marketing strategy, which taught me a very different philosophy in contrast to this Guiding Principle. After I started to understand Vibrational Marketing, it felt like a brain twister to try and process. I couldn't easily wrap my head around the understanding that <u>my ideal clients had already been gathered for me</u>, and that aspect of my business wasn't actually my responsibility. The truth is that I believed it was my responsibility, and so my journey to accepting and living by this Guiding Principle has taken some serious reprogramming.

In addition, with increased exposure to so many marketing experts and gurus all sharing their methods of attracting clients and building "seven figure businesses," there were many times in my journey when I got distracted and confused. I bought into the belief that these other well-meaning individuals and rock star marketing experts knew more precisely how to market my business products and services. In many ways, I desperately wanted to believe that if I followed their prescribed methods, then I'd have the magic formula for endless client attraction, which is what many of them promised, and I foolishly believed.

In retrospect, I now understand why that pathway just doesn't provide consistent results. I presently recognize that from a vibrational perspective, each person who has obtained success in his or her business by taking certain actions, experienced that level of success not because of a formula, or the specific series of actions taken, but <u>because the</u>

entrepreneur was in alignment with his or her desires. The entrepreneur felt good and took inspired action; and because of it, he or she experienced great success. It wasn't the marketing method that equalled the results, it was one's vibrational alignment that made the difference.

What this realization equates to is that there really isn't a guaranteed marketing or sales formula that will work for everyone. There are no rigorous courses or enchanted strategies to complete. A magic pill solution, clever strategy, or fairy-tale funnel hack that can guarantee results just doesn't exist.

What does exist is my own guidance system, that tells me in every moment how I'm feeling. I can tune to my guidance system as I work on and in my business, listen for inspiration, and take inspired action based on it feeling good to me. This approach offers the most effective type of marketing strategy.

VIBRATIONAL ADVERTISEMENT

A reference that applies these understandings into perspective is when I think about myself as radiating out a vibrational advertisement for my business. Again, since I'm the vibrational Being that influences my business the most, my vibration impacts the success and results of my business. When I consider the vibrational advertisement I'm signalling out into the Universe, it's not so much about what this advertisement says, or its appearance, that's most important; on the contrary, what's most critical is how my vibrational advertisement feels. What feelings are evoked within me by my vibrational advertisement?

What emotions do my vibrational advertisement radiate to others? Who will be attracted to my vibrational advertisement because someone is seeking that same feeling?

As the vibrational advertisement flows out of me, I imagine it being like a bright beacon of light radiating out from the center of my heart. This beautiful bright light shines and sends vibrational waves out into the Universe. Other vibrational Beings who are seeking the same feelings as my vibrational advertisement, will naturally gravitate towards it.

By offering a vibrational advertisement that's in alignment with Source Energy, I allow the ideal clients to flow to me, by shining a bright beautiful light that they can gravitate towards.

I signal out that I'm "vibrationally open for business. My vibrational advertisement is the final piece in my allowing, and it's based on how I feel. When I feel good, when I feel excited about what I'm sharing with the world, when I feel in love with what I'm delivering, and when I feel eager and excited to share these offerings with others, my vibrational advertisement is shining bright. Results are guaranteed. It's the Law.

WHICH MARKETING EFFORTS FEEL GOOD TO ME?

An effective practice for Vibrational Marketing is to focus on all that I love and enjoy about the products and services I'm offering. Creating lists within my journal of what I love and appreciate most about them, how effective they are, how much fun it is for me to offer them, and how much of an impact I know they have on uplifting others. Writing about all the things I love about my product and service offerings makes me feel good, and so this practice is a wonderful way for me to get into vibrational alignment with my business desires.

Once I feel in alignment, I can spend time contemplating how I'd like to share about my products and services. Which methods of communicating actually feel good to me? Which communication strategies with my ideal clients do I actually enjoy? For example, I personally enjoy focusing my marketing efforts on leading with value and knowledge. I often provide trainings, webinars, and other opportunities for prospective clients to receive valuable guidance as a method of getting familiar with my work.

It's when I specifically choose marketing tactics and approaches based on **my** enjoyment of them, I successfully maintain my vibrational alignment; which means I am vibrating on a frequency that will allow the receiving of my desires. When I select marketing tactics and approaches based on what others have influenced or told me are effective (but I give no consideration to how those approaches make me feel as I execute them), I often find myself misaligned and uninspired.

Personal Reminder: There isn't a right or wrong way for me to market my products and services. As long as I'm following my inner guidance and listening to what feels good, whatever approaches I take will be effective. There isn't a predetermined formula for how many messages to share, where I should share those messages, or what those messages should say or look like. The only consideration I must factor in is, do I feel good sharing in this way? In fact, there are many examples of highly successful businesses that seemly do next to no external marketing or promoting at all. I've experienced it personally: how someone who offers a valuable, uplifting, and impactful service seems to naturally attract an abundance of clients, without much outward effort or focus on marketing. Plus, I know through my own experiences that it's not about the quantity, methods, latest technologies, and/or most sophisticated funnel or sales system. Vibration and expectation of success are what matter most.

LISTENING TO MY GUIDANCE AS I STEP OUT OF MY COMFORT ZONE

As I sift and sort through the wide variety of marketing approaches, tactics, and methods for communicating with others about my products and services, I acknowledge that there may be an element of uneasiness when I contemplate and consider trying a new approach. The first few times I did a live broadcast, I felt an element of discomfort, the same happened with sharing videos and presenting in live seminars. Yet my uneasiness was only a result of stepping outside of my comfort zone, so I accept that it was merely my natural stress response kicking in and presenting fear as I moved into unchartered territory.

As I feel the temptation to pull back and shrink into my comfort zone because of fear, it benefits me to pause in those moments and listen for inner guidance. I can ask Source Energy if what I'm feeling is a result of temporary fear caused by trying something new, or is it guidance telling me this marketing approach simply doesn't feel good, isn't fun, and is causing me a lot of stress? Clarity is consistently revealed in the silence, and even as I test and try different marketing approaches, I tune to this guidance.

I'm hardwired with a guidance system that sends me signals based on my vibration. I have only to listen and tune to this guidance to know which path is best for me to take.

As I embrace the wisdom of Guiding Principle No. 7, I now let fun lead the way as much as I can in my marketing efforts. As I shared before, my educational background from Business School, and my conditioned beliefs about marketing and sales have made practicing this Guiding Principle something that I have to do very deliberately now. Prior to creating a social media post or promotion, or sharing about my business in any way, I try to remember to ask myself: Why I am about to take this action? Is it because I want to, and it feels fun to me? Or is it because deep down inside I still mistakenly believe I have to do this? Am I allowing my guidance to lead the way, or is old programming leading the way? Am I trying to attempt to do the job of the Universe by drawing ideal clients to me, or am I focusing on feeling good and aligning my vibration so the Universe can bring forward those ideal clients? When I pause to ask myself these questions, it's still surprising how often I discover my action was being motivated by outside influence and old conditioned beliefs about marketing and sales.

Through practice and repetition, this ability will become more automatic and natural.

REFLECTING ON GUIDING PRINCIPLE NO. 7

Q. What do I enjoy and appreciate the most about the products and services I'm offering within my business?

Q. Am I "vibrationally open for business" right now? If so, what would I like my vibrational advertisement to feel like?

Q. How do I personally like to share about my products and services? What methods of communicating actually feel good to me? What methods of communicating with my ideal clients do I actually enjoy?

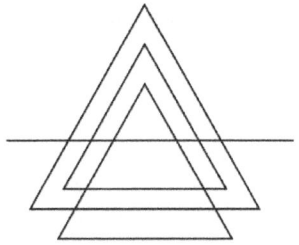

GUIDING PRINCIPLE NO. 8:

THE KEY TO MY VIBRATIONAL BUSINESS STRATEGY IS TO FEEL GOOD.

My most valuable contribution isn't the action that I take, but instead the vibration I offer. By aligning with Source Energy, I harness the most powerful Law in the Universe, and I magnify the impact and the outcome of all I pursue.

WILLINGNESS

The most significant question I can pose to myself is: how willing am I? How willing am I to look at my business through this expanded vibrational lens?

Am I open to following my emotional guidance system, and in doing so, evolve my business strategy to center around me, and how I feel?

The truth is that this decision takes a tremendous amount of courage. The answer becomes immensely clear when I remind myself of the physical Beings I am inspired to help uplift and serve through the avenue of my business. For them and for myself, I AM willing. As an extension of Source Energy, here in this physical experience as a creator and an uplifter, I am willing to expand. Evolving my level of consciousness as an entrepreneur presents the opportunity to co-create with Universal forces. In turn, this transformation is the pathway to fulfill my greatest desire for impact, enrichment, and joy.

REVOLVING MY BUSINESS AROUND ME, NOT MY IDEAL CUSTOMER

For much of my early years of entrepreneurship, I allowed the concept of my ideal client or client avatar to take the center stage of my business strategy. All of the processes, systems, and strategies I implemented in my business aimed at attracting, serving, and pleasing my ideal clients. This mentality was, in fact, precisely what I'd been taught in Business School. Besides, all the business resources, trainings, and programs I'd taken to further my education in business also mirrored these same recommendations: "The customer is the center of my business Universe" and "the customer is always right" were the undeniable truths that were ingrained at every level of my business strategy.

My fatal flaw in this business philosophy of course, was that the customer wasn't always right. In fact, by prioritizing others' needs before my own, and trying to jump through hoops to make others happy at the sacrifice of myself, I unconsciously allowed my vibration to lower. Accordingly, my business results reflected how I felt on the inside. I now understand that when I revolve my business strategy around me (the entrepreneur and vibrational Being who influences my business the most), and I prioritize my alignment and good feeling emotions, the Law of Attraction will easily and effortlessly bring forward my ideal clients without me having to make personal sacrifices in order to receive them.

The pathway to success always begins with my vibrational alignment.

VIBRATIONAL LEADERSHIP

As I weave the wisdom from within these pages into my business strategy, I can identify areas of opportunity to revisit and revamp within my business operations. As the leader of my company, the processes and practices I use to recruit, screen, interview, and on-board team members should feel in alignment with me. This unity also transcends into all of the aspects of leading my team: The methods I utilize to communicate and give instructions and guidance; the approaches I embrace for leading team meetings; the ways in which I approach conflict resolution; the mission and vision I set for my company. All aspects of my leadership decision making should hinge on my vibrational alignment, ensuring I continue to feel good as I work on and in my business.

WHO DO I DESIRE TO PLAY WITH?

Putting myself in the center of my business strategy permits me to have a lot of fun in the Creation Process. I can begin by asking myself pleasing questions such as: Who do I truly want to interact with as clients? What type of clients would be enjoyable and rewarding to welcome into my business? How do I want our interactions to play out? How do I want the sales process to unfold with them? What kinds of experiences do I want to have with them? How do I want our relationship to unfold? What do I look forward to most in working with them? What will inspire and motivate me about them?

As I continue to remind myself that feeling good is my number one priority, and I take time to write out answers to these questions, I'm transmitting clear desires to Source Energy (Step 1). Source Energy answers my desires (Step 2) and these ideal clients are instantly created, attracted, gathered, and assembled. The Universe matches my good feeling vibrations with the good feeling vibrations of these ideal clients, and I allow the receiving of them (Step 3).

Being playful, having fun, feeling good, and managing my vibrational point of attraction illuminates the pathway to allow an abundance of ideal clients into my business.

Experiencing success in business is, in fact, much easier and more pleasurable than I've often allowed myself to believe in the past.

REDEFINING MY WORK SCHEDULE

Embracing a vibrational business strategy allows me the opportunity to explore my working schedule with permission to redefine what "working" actually means to me. I can reflect on questions such as: Where do I enjoy working from? Does a beautifully decorated office feel good to me, or do I prefer a laptop lifestyle where I can work from anywhere in the world? Or do I desire the flexibility of having both options? Does it feel good to have a set working schedule with pre-determined hours, <u>or</u> does it feel better to reach for alignment everyday, and then allow inspiration to influence when I'll work and for how long? Can I allow alignment and feeling good to be the gauge that signals when it's time to take a break? Also what projects and activities do I desire to spend the vast majority of my working hours performing? What tasks bring me the absolute most amount of pleasure in my business?

One of the most powerful questions I can begin asking myself is: If time and money were unlimited *(which they are)*, and if other people's opinions didn't matter to me, what would my working schedule look and feel like?

IT TAKES COURAGE TO BE SELFISH

I was raised to be anything but selfish. On the contrary, one of the goals I strived for most in my life, was to make others feel good. The more joy I experienced from pleasing others, the more I strived to please, even if it translated into occasionally sacrificing my joy for the sake of others joy. I valued giving to others much more than pleasing myself, and I carried this value well into my adult years. It wasn't until I started to fully understand vibration, that I finally started to see the downfall of a lifetime of giving, without often factoring my feelings into the mix.

As I embrace the wisdom of Guiding Principle No. 8, I acknowledge that it takes a lot of personal courage to begin embracing selfishness. The very definition of selfish is, "to be concerned chiefly with one's own personal profit or pleasure," and knowing what I now know about Universal Law, the Creation Process, manifestation, and vibration - that's exactly what I need to be cultivating in order to be the powerful creator that I am.

I absolutely need to be chiefly concerned about my own profit and pleasure, but here's the part that I used to get caught up on - my profit and pleasure doesn't have to be at the expense of anyone else's profit and pleasure. I can release the false premise of competition because my success doesn't in any way take away from anyone else. The Universe is limitless and infinitely abundant. As physical Beings, we're all here as powerful creators. We all have the ability to create whatever it is that we desire. We're not here to compete for what has already been created, as expansion calls much more from us.

REFLECTING ON GUIDING PRINCIPLE NO. 8

Q. Am I willing to be selfish? Am I open to following my emotional guidance system; and in doing so, evolve my business strategy to center around me and how I feel?

Q. In what areas of my business can I infuse the strategy of feeling good, to ensure my overall experience as the entrepreneur, business owner, and leader of my company is enjoyable and fun?

FINAL THOUGHTS AND SUMMATION

Congratulations on journeying through this Personal Guidebook. Like a lotus flower you have opened yourself up to new perspectives and ways of viewing yourself and your business. It's likely that some of the concepts and ideas presented oppose your existing beliefs about business, money, and the keys to being successful as a business owner.

My sincerest desire is that despite any inner chatter you may have experienced, you also felt a strong resonance with the key messages and Guiding Principles. My suggestion is to revisit this resource repeatedly, as each opportunity of processing will allow the wisdom contained within these pages to seep further into your inner knowing. Over time, you'll find yourself opening up to the importance of practicing and managing your vibrational alignment in business. As you focus on feeling good throughout your business journey, your power to create, uplift, and allow also increases. May you come to know just how capable of magnificence you truly are.

As a reminder: for those seeking additional guidance regarding the practical application of the Principles contained within this Guidebook, my recommendation is to build upon this resource with the companion, **Business of Vibration Online Masterclass Program**.

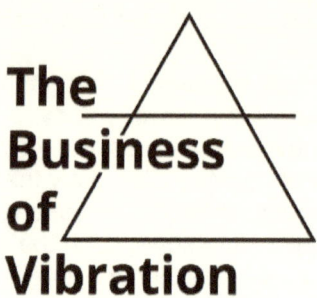

The Business of Vibration

This online Masterclass compliments the Guiding Principles contained within this book with further in-depth coaching and practical guidance. For additional information on the Business of Vibration Online Masterclass Program, visit:

www.dawnwotherspoon.com/thebusinessofvibration

ACKNOWLEDGMENTS

I co-created this resource with Source Energy, and I'd like to express my deepest gratitude for this incredible opportunity. It has been my absolute honor!

There are also many beautiful souls who I would like to thank for their abundance of support in the writing of this book.

First and foremost, I thank my husband Morgan, who has stood by my side through the years of immense spiritual growth, soul searching, and professional development. Inner evolution and expansion inherently creates an environment of uncertainty, and throughout all of my personal growth, you've provided the stability and steadiness our family has needed. For that, and for the love that you've shared with our girls and me, I am eternally grateful to you, my soul partner.

I thank my girls, Ella and Sadie. You've been a constant source of light and playfulness, always reminding me that this life experience is a precious gift to be enjoyed. Thank you for your unconditional love, for choosing me as your mother, and for being the most profound examples of Source Energy's love here in the physical. I love you forever!

To all of my extended family, including my parents Violet and Stan Predinchuk, parents-in-law Barb and Rod Wotherspoon, sister Marcy, Greg, Olivia, and Grace Cylka, Brother-in-law Chris, Kim, Broden, Reid and Jaxon Wotherspoon, Brother-in-law Blaine, Rochelle, Dade and Hudsyn Wotherspoon, and Brother-in-law Eric and Adele Wotherspoon *(and their puppy Ophelia)*, thank you for your love and support over the years. I can attest that it truly "takes a village" to successfully raise a family, pursue this crazy path of entrepreneurship, and also embrace my gifts as a writer and author, so I thank you for always being here as our support system.

Thank you to my soul sisters, and fellow coaches and mentors who supported me through the writing of this book: Amanda Skiles, Bev Lazar, Danielle Debay, Lucy Pritchett, Angela Claybourn, Dani McDonald, Jami Young, Jeannine Yoder, Janelle Nice, and Kelly Hayes. Words cannot adequately express how much the sisterhood you've shown me has expanded my capacity to love. Thank you for all you've contributed to my life.

Thank you to my beautiful movement and wellness business {ClubMynx}, to my team of beautiful Instructors, the many clients, and community supporters who've rallied around me over the years in support of that beautiful business - I am forever grateful. To my coaching clients past and present, and to all the readers and raving fans, I thank you for inspiring me to step into the fullness of who I am meant to be.

I'd also like to thank the many incredible spiritual teachers, insightful authors, and fascinating coaches who've been inspirational and influential in an abundance of ways throughout the course of my life. **Most significantly, I'd like to recognize the profound teachings of Esther and Jerry Hicks (The Teachings of Abraham) for decades worth of invaluable wisdom sharing**. Much of what I now know to be true at the depths of my Being, has been cultivated by your teachings, and so I thank you from the bottom of my heart.

To my editor, Stacy Shaneyfelt, you're brilliant and I'm grateful for your support and guidance with transforming this book into a masterpiece.

There are also many others who've been a beacon of light in my life, and my sincere hope is that you know who are, and just how special you are to me… from all that I am, I thank you!

Dawn Wotherspoon

ABOUT THE AUTHOR

Dawn Wotherspoon is a modern day spiritual entrepreneur and an avid student of the Natural Laws of the Universe. She is a Spiritual Business Coach, Meditation Teacher, and the creator of the signature programs: **Sacred Self**, **Discovering Greatness Within**, and **The Business of Vibration**. Throughout her various roles, Dawn's primary aim is to help those who are activated for purposeful work, connect with their natural confidence, and master their creative powers, so they can step into the fullness of who they are truly meant to be.

For details on her various programs and courses visit: www.DawnWotherspoon.com.